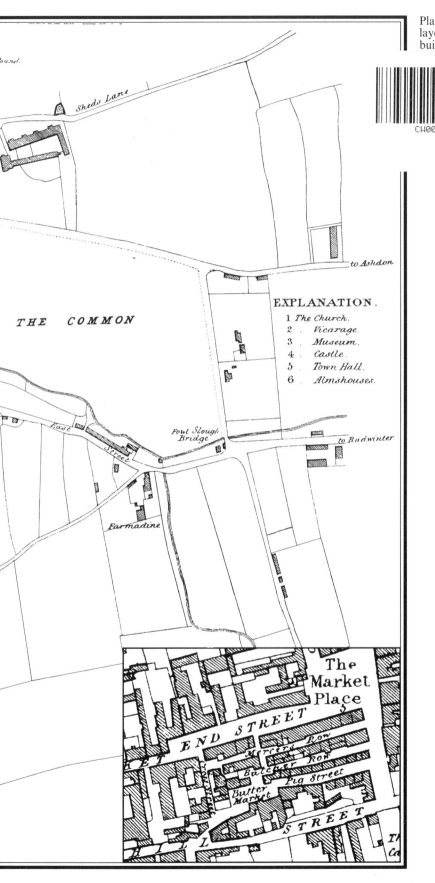

Plan of Saffron Walden in 1835. The layout of streets and siting of the buildings were strongly influenced by 'le and its many of the as Cucking troduction) t rows are

EXPLANATION.

1 The Church.
2 . Vicarage.
3 . Museum.
4 . Castle.
5 . Town Hall.
6 . Almshouses.

SAFFRON WALDEN
A Pictorial History

High Street, 1930.

SAFFRON WALDEN
A Pictorial History

**Martyn Everett
and
Howard Newman**

Phillimore

1998

Published by
PHILLIMORE & CO. LTD.,
Shopwyke Manor Barn, Chichester, West Sussex

© Martyn Everett and Howard Newman, 1998

ISBN 0 85033 951 0

Printed and bound in Great Britain by
BIDDLES LTD.
Guildford, Surrey

This book is dedicated to
Zosia and Staszek Everett
and to
Inge and Joshua Newman

List of Illustrations

Frontispiece: High Street, 1930

Preface and Acknowledgements

Without the knowledge, help and assistance of many people over several years, this book could not have been written, and so the authors would like to thank the following: Olive Newman, Ena Wright, Zofia Everett, Inge Newman, Martin Turnbull of Harts Ltd., Len Pole, Sir Henry Marking, everyone at Saffron Walden Museum, and all the staff at Saffron Walden Library. The readers who use Saffron Walden Library should also be mentioned, because the flow of information has always been a two-way process, and in addition to provoking constant further enquiry, they have transformed work into pleasure. Without the work of local photographers, since the 19th century, this book would not have been possible. In particular we would like to thank David Campbell whose photographs provide a lasting record of the town in more recent times, and John Clayden. We also wish to acknowledge all those past and present historians of Saffron Walden whose work provided the foundation for our own book, including Stephen Bassett; Richard, Lord Braybrooke; Mrs. D. Cromarty; C. B. Rowntree; Cliff Stacey; Malcolm White and Mary Whiteman.

Introduction

Prehistoric Settlement

The small market town of Saffron Walden lies in the remote north-west corner of Essex, on the gentle slopes of the Upper Cam valley. Archaeological evidence suggests that the valley has been inhabited from at least the Neolithic period onwards, when it was an ancient trackway. Worked flints have been found on the well-drained glacial gravel terraces at Newport, Wenden, Littlebury and Great Chesterford. The clay soils of the wooded upland slopes were less attractive to prehistoric settlement, except at Saffron Walden, where some Mesolithic tools and large quantities of worked flints from the Neolithic period have been found.

Excavations at Elm Grove in Saffron Walden have demonstrated the existence of Iron-Age settlement, and large collections of worked flints have also been found near the Battle Ditches, and in Abbey Lane. Neolithic and Iron-Age pottery has been found at a number of these sites, and a small but significant group of flints has also been found at Castle Meadow.

In the late 19th century construction workers uncovered a series of pits containing decayed red deer antlers to the north of West Road, and in the early 20th century a 'well-defined and deep trench' over 200 metres long, containing at one point two or three skeletons 'evidently thrown into the trench in haste on top of one another', was found in Mount Pleasant Road, suggesting the existence of a Neolithic causewayed enclosure. Prehistoric ditches have also been observed under the southern arm of Myddylton Place, and near Raynham's Garage, High Street.

Close to the town, near Audley End mansion, is an oval single-ramparted contour fort, the Ring Hill Camp, and at Grimsditch Wood, along the Little Walden Road, there is an irregular enclosure consisting of a single rampart and ditch, enclosing a cigar-shaped mound, which might be a barrow. Both these earthworks are believed by archaeologists to relate to Bronze-Age settlement.

The Romano-British Settlement

The small number and scattered nature of archaeological finds from the Roman period have suggested to archaeologists the existence of a small Romano-British settlement, including a small Roman fort, garrisoned from the much larger Roman town of Cestreforda, now known as Great Chesterford.

This fort was probably located on, or near, the site of a later Anglo-Saxon cemetery in Abbey Lane. Certainly some of the burials in this cemetery are Romano-British, dating from the third or fourth centuries. A second smaller Roman settlement, again with a military purpose, was established at Little Walden, associated with the construction of a Roman road to Cestreforda. Aerial photographs reveal another Roman road running along the floor of the Granta valley, passing Wendens Ambo, the site of a Roman villa, and close to Audley End mansion.

The Romano-British settlement was eventually replaced by Germanic settlers, invading from the north and gradually settling the Cam Valley. Many local field names originate from this period, and suggest that the new inhabitants were Saxon although some of the fields and hamlets possess Danish names. Historians have suggested that the name Walden originates from this period and is derived from the Old English 'Weala-denu', the valley of Britains or serfs, implying the continued existence of a community populated by the indigenous inhabitants rather than Anglo-Saxons.

Domesday Book

When Domesday Book was compiled by the Norman conquerors in 1086 they provided the following description of the settlement:

Hund de Vdelesforda. Waledanā ten&.G.in dn̄io.qđ ten Anfgar.t.r.e.p Man.7 p xviiii.hiđ.7.dim.Tē 7 p̄ viii.car in dn̄io.m.x. Sēp xxii.car hom.Tē 7 p̄.lxvi.uiłt.m̄ xlvi. Tē 7 p̄ xvii.bord.m̄.xl.Tē 7 p̄.xvi.fer.m̄.xx.Tē 7 p̄ filua .m̄.porc.m̄.ɒccc.7.lxxx.ac.p̄ti.Sēp.i.mot. huic manerio adjacebant.t.r.e.xiii.foc.m̄.xiiii.tenentes.vi.&.dimiđ hiđ	Geoffrey holds Waledana in lordship, which Ansgar held before 1066 as a manor, for 19½ hides. Then and later 8 ploughs in lordship, now 10. Always 22 men's ploughs. Then and later 66 villagers, now 46, then and later 17 smallholders, now 40, then and later 16 slaves, now 20. Woodland, then and later 1000 pigs, now 800; meadow, 80 acres; always 1 mill.
Tē 7 poſt.viii.car 7 dim.m̄.viii.Tē 7 p̄.x.bord.m̄.xiiii.Tē 7 p̄ filu. .l.porc.m̄.xxx.xx.ac p̄ti.tēia pars molini.Tē.vi.runc.xi...im. .cc.ou.cx.porc.xl.cap.iiii.uafa apū.m̄.ix.runc.x.an.ccxliii.ou. .c.porc.xx.cap.xxx.uafa apū.Tē 7 p̄ uał.xxxvi.lib.m̄ uał.l.lib.	Attached to this manor before 1066 were 13 freemen, now 14, who hold 6½ hides. Then and later 50 pigs, now 30; meadow, 20 acres; the third part of a mill. then 6 cobs, 11 cattle, 200 sheep, 110 pigs, 40 goats, 4 beehives; now 9 cobs, 10 cattle, 243 sheep, 100 pigs, 20 goats, 30 beehives.
	Value then and later £36; value now £50.
De hoc manerio ten&.Odo.i.hiđ.7.i.uirḡ.7 Renald.i.hiđ.xii.ac. min.7.ii.car.7.xiii.bord.7 uał.l.fol in eod p̄tio.	Of this manor, Odo holds 1 hide and 1 virgate and Reginald (holds) 1 hide less 12 acres. 2 ploughs.
	13 smallholders.
	Value 50s in the same assessment.

From this entry we can see that Walden was held before the Conquest by Ansgar, as a manor of 19½ hides or about 2,200 acres. Ansgar was a powerful and wealthy man, sheriff of the Middle Saxons, and the king's standard-bearer, who owned land throughout Essex. Descended from a follower of King Cnut, his father founded Waltham Abbey. Ansgar was badly injured at the Battle of Hastings, and had to be carried to London, where in spite of his wounds he attempted to rally the Anglo-Saxons and pretended to negotiate with William the Conqueror, but William outwitted Ansgar, who was imprisoned and died from his injuries.

Ansgar's Essex lands were given to Geoffrey de Mandeville (I), first constable of the Tower of London. This Geoffrey had a grandson, also called Geoffrey, who after succession to the title in 1130 also became constable of the Tower of London. Geoffrey de Mandeville (II) transformed the Anglo-Saxon settlement of *Waldena* into the nucleus of the modern town, building the castle on Bury Hill at some time between 1125 and 1141 and founding the Priory of St James, later the Abbey of Walden, in about 1139.

Following the death of King Henry I in 1135, England was plunged into civil war when the king's nephew, Stephen, claimed the throne from the rightful heir, Henry's daughter, the Empress Maud. Geoffrey de Mandeville (II) supported Stephen at first, and was rewarded with the Earldom of Essex, but in the following year he changed his allegiance, when Maud, to gain his support, gave him a charter, permitting him to move the market then held in Newport 'into his castle at Walden'. This market was located inside the castle bailey, roughly on the site of the present High Street, between Church Street and Castle Street. When the Close, an old timber-framed building which stood between the church and High Street, was demolished in the 1930s, part of the old stone Market Cross was discovered beneath the foundations. The Sunday market and a week long fair at Pentecost stimulated the growth of a new community around the castle.

Soon Geoffrey changed sides again, accepting a large annual income from Stephen, and the right to have 60 knights in his train but, when he conspired with Maud to change sides once more, Stephen had him arrested while attending court in St Albans. Geoffrey was offered the stark choice of giving up his position as constable at the tower and surrendering his castles at Pleshey and Walden, or being hanged. Geoffrey surrendered his castles, and was released, although the king might have saved trouble by hanging him, as in revenge Geoffrey went into outright rebellion against Stephen. He gathered an army and attacked Ely, Ramsey Abbey, and then Cambridge, which was loyal to the king, massacring the people and setting the city on fire. Soon afterwards Geoffrey was struck by a chance arrow during a skirmish near Burwell, and died two days later in September 1144. Excommunicated for his attacks on church property, he was denied burial at Walden Priory. According to the contemporary chronicle *Gesta Stephani*, his body was carried to London, where it was 'hung in a lead coffin upon a tree in the old Temple Church garden'.

Almost immediately Walden was the scene of a second rebellion against the king. Soon after Geoffrey de Mandeville's death King Stephen entrusted Walden Castle to the guardianship of Turgis d'Avranches, a favourite of Stephen's who had risen from a poor, humble Norman family. When the king wanted to enter the castle, Turgis refused, fearing his position might be given to someone else. Stephen returned without warning accompanied by a strong body of knights, while Turgis was hunting with dogs. Cut off from the castle, Turgis was forced to surrender.

Walden Abbey

Geoffrey de Mandeville (II) founded the Benedictine monastery of St James as a priory, sometime between 1139 and the end of 1143. It was situated at Brookwalden, just outside Walden, at what is now Audley End village. The chosen site was a narrow area of land:

> flat and four-sided, fairly free from filth, with healthy air for those dwelling there, watered by streams which rise and flow there perpetually, at no time failing. It receives the rays of the rising sun rather late, and loses those of the setting sun rather early, hills being interposed on either side.

Geoffrey chose this site, near the intersection of four main roads, so that the monks might provide hospitality to wayfarers, and still be close to his castle. In addition he endowed the priory with tithes and property of the church of Walden, and 19 other churches, a mill at Walden, and woodlands and meadows.

1 *Above left.* The seal of William de Mandeville, who gave half the manor of Walden to Walden Abbey.

2 *Above right.* Seals of Walden Abbey. The cockleshells on the seals were the emblem of St James, to whom the abbey was dedicated.

The first Prior, William, erected a small dwelling for two or three monks outside the consecrated area, 'near their own mill ... between the stream and the public road'. Within a short time a new site was chosen, and eventually a third and final site where the monks built

> a wooden chapel of a humble nature with a cloister and outbuildings, a hall with a chamber, a bakery, a stable, with very small granaries, a garden, a shrubbery; a very small pond, a ditch all around the cemetery, with new walls to the monastry, of stone indeed, but neither high nor broad, belonging to the presbytery, and wings on both sides, with one altar, and besides this a small house, with a little barn nearby the clearing.

The second prior, Reginald, was responsible for moving many of the buildings to higher ground, and for building a new cloister and chapter 'more suitably constructed'. Later the monks 'raised a tower beyond the choir upon arches, with a wooden structure placed above, raised to a height and fitted with a bell'.

The building of the abbey and the granting of a Tuesday market in 1295 resulted in the growth of a small settlement in its vicinity, so that by 1400 a survey of the abbey lands noted that a shop, 51 houses on two streets, with other dwellings nearby, had grown up around the abbey.

Life for the monks at the abbey was far from trouble-free. Neither of Geoffrey de Mandeville's sons had any family, and there were rival claimants to the inheritance. Sir Geoffrey Fitzpiers eventually succeeded, after paying 7,000 marks to King Richard. Fitzpiers resented the abbey, which had received bequests from William de Mandeville, which had the effect of reducing the size of Fitzpiers' eventual inheritance. He forbade the abbey to occupy any of the lands granted to them, and sent almost one hundred of his own ploughmen to plough the abbey fields. This dispute escalated during the next seven years. Park fencing was destroyed and abbey lands plundered, while monks from the abbey were ambushed and beaten on their way to market in Walden. Abbey servants were placed in the stocks and beaten, and some servants were even killed. Animals and ploughmen from the abbey were attacked, and the livestock seized and held in Walden Castle for ransom.

At one point Fitzpiers men, 'The unquiet clients of Satan', committed:

> a deed of horror, which had never been heard of before among the nations ... for they suspended the [sheep's] corpses, which had turned through excessive corruption into noisesomeness, on the tops of the [castle] walls, and thus raised them high, so as to infect the air, which at the time was very calm, with the putridity ...

By the time of the dissolution of the monasteries, the monks appeared to have forgotten their original purpose. A separate residence had been built for the abbot, several miles from the abbey, at St Aylotts, near Sewards End. Robert Barrington, the last but one abbot of Walden, fought a losing battle against the temptations of the flesh. In 1534 he was granted a dispensation that he and four other monks could sit at the same table and eat flesh, butter, eggs, cheese and other milk foods on fast days, when such foods were normally forbidden to monks. During the Visitation of 1535 Barrington confessed that he had secretly married a Mistress Bures, a nun of the Minoresses. He offered to surrender the abbey, as there were only seven monks remaining, all elderly—a rapid decline in numbers, as 18 monks and the abbot had repudiated the pope the year before. Although the third largest religious house in Essex, it was only the sixth richest in terms of income per head. Within five days of the abbey and its lands being surrendered to the king, they were granted to Sir Thomas Audley who converted the abbey buildings into a residence. After Audley's death the property descended to Thomas Howard, who became Earl of Suffolk in 1603, the same year in which he started to build the palace at Audley End. The abbey was completely demolished, but its foundations were incorporated into the new building, which retained much of the layout of the abbey cloisters. Little remains of the original abbey apart from the old hostel, now referred to as the stables, and the old abbey hospital at St Marks in Audley End village. The latter is not the original building, which was demolished and replaced by almshouses built in the footprint of the earlier building.

Medieval Saffron Walden

Archaeological evidence suggests that the Anglo-Saxon settlement in Abbey Lane continued on the same site, while the new town grew up on Bury Hill. Changes inside the castle bailey considerably altered the shape of the original Norman settlement. The main road from Newport to Cambridge, which passed to the west of the town (between the Battle Ditches and the existing Park wall) and joined the existing road near the top of Windmill Hill, was re-routed through the castle bailey, displacing the market from its original location to create High Street. The church in Abbey Lane (probably a wooden structure) was replaced by a new church on Bury Hill, and the market was re-established on the south side of Bury Hill but to the north of the King's Ditch.

It was at about this time that the earliest earthworks on the south and east of the castle were levelled, and the massive but wrongly-named Battle Ditches were constructed. For a long time the ditches, more properly called the *magnum fossatum*, were believed to be prehistoric, but archaeological investigation in the 1970s demonstrated that they were constructed between about 1227 and 1240, in order to delineate the boundaries of the town. Land enclosed by the ditches was divided into regular plots in the hope of facilitating expansion of the town, but the growth never materialised. Construction of the ditches probably resulted in the final displacement of the Anglo-Saxon settlement, as the western ditch passed right through its centre.

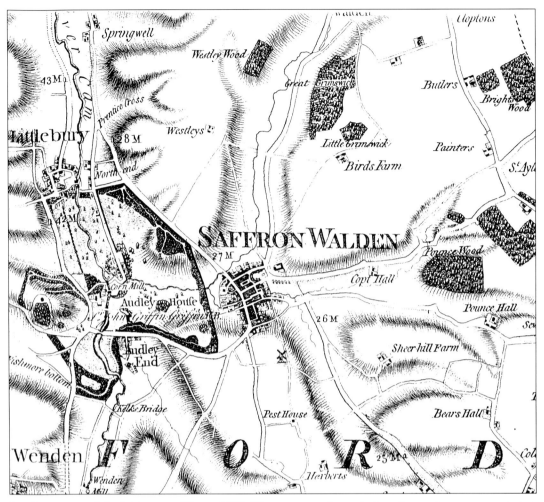

3 Chapman and Andrés' map of Essex, 1777. The map was drawn before the roads were re-routed at Audley End, and shows the position of the cornmill mentioned in Domesday Book, which later belonged to the monks at Walden Abbey. It also demonstrates the hills which were an important factor in the siting of the Norman castle.

According to historian and contemporary chronicler Matthew Paris, Saffron Walden was the location of a grand tournament in 1252. During this tournament, one of the knights, Roger de Leeburn, encountered another knight, Ernauld de Mounteney. He 'ran his lance into his throat under the helmet, it wanting a collar, whereupon Mounteney fell from his horse and died.' Paris reports that it was widely believed that Roger deliberately killed Ernauld in revenge for a broken leg received at an earlier contest.

In 1295 the market expanded to include a Tuesday market, and in about 1300 the town was awarded a charter by the de Bohun's which relieved the inhabitants of heriot, marking an important break with the feudal system, and contributing to the town's growing prosperity. During this period the town was often known as Chepynge (or Chipping, from a word meaning a market) Walden, reflecting the importance of the market.

The economy of 14th-century Britain was disrupted by the Black Death. Walden was no exception, although there is no record of the impact of Black Death on the town, but the high death toll resulted in food shortages, high prices and a scarcity of labour. King and Parliament enacted a 'Statute of Labourers' in an attempt to control wages. A few years later the added burden of a series of poll-taxes to finance the war in France proved intolerable, and led to the Peasants' Revolt in 1381.

The absence of court rolls for Saffron Walden before 1381 suggests their destruction during the rebellion, but there is no other evidence of the impact of the revolt on the town, apart from a single reference in the court rolls of April 1384, where there is mention of the 'rolls of the court, with other deeds and charters of the Lord [which] were burnt in the time of ruin'. Certainly many of the immediately surrounding villages took part in the revolt. Thomas Hasilden's manor at Little Chesterford was attacked and looted, and other manors were attacked at Clavering, Debden, Widdington, Wimbish and elsewhere, and documents were burnt.

In 1400 the Guild of Our Lady of Pity was formed in order to provide an almshouse for the 'succor and sustenance of XIII poor men such as be lame, crooked, blind and bedridden, and most in need'. The guild provided a house in the churchyard for the priest who was to act as a chaplain to the almshouse, and encouraged local priests to start a school, but in 1423 John de Hatfield, the Abbot of Walden, summoned the two priests, John Bernard and William Brynge, and accused them of teaching without the abbot's authority. As a concession they were allowed to teach Greek, but nothing else.

During the late 14th and early 15th centuries the town's wealth derived principally from wool, although malting and brewing were already providing a living for many people. The abbot of Walden had over 400 sheep and, although the abbey restricted ownership by its tenants, there were over 2,300 sheep listed in the returns of local landowners in 1419, usually in large flocks numbering between 160 and 300 sheep. At first, it was trade in the animals and their 'golden fleece' that was important but, with the expansion of the wool trade in the late 14th century, dyeworks were established around the castle bailey, and cloth was woven and dyed in the town. The woollen industry thrived, and eventually the local woolstaplers built their own guild hall in the market place, which survived until it was demolished in 1847 to make way for the Corn Exchange. One of the most important annual festivals was the woolstaplers' picturesque procession round the town. Led by Bishop Blaize, their patron saint, the woolstaplers dressed in brightly dyed woollen robes and feathered hats processed around

4 Walden Castle in 1787. Constructed some time between 1125 and 1143, it was partly demolished in *c.*1157 when £9 12s. 0d. was collected for 'throwing down Earl Geoffrey's castles in Essex'. Rebuilt *c.*1170, the facing stones were removed in the mid-13th century for use in the foundations of the new church. It was heavily plundered as a source of building materials during the 16th century.

5 Sheep grazing on Castle Meadow, 1930. The small turret was added by Lord Howard de Walden in 1796 to enable a signal beacon to be lit from it in the event of a French invasion.

the town, accompanied by the chamberlain and the Corporation, a noisy band, young shepherds and shepherdesses carrying lambs. Even as late as 1700 about half the population was employed in the wool trade, and the procession itself continued until 1778.

Saffron

Wool was soon overtaken by the saffron industry as the main source of local wealth, and it is from the autumn-flowering saffron crocus that Walden derives its name. According to the legend recounted by the Dutch writer Hakluyt, a pilgrim:

> ... stole a head of saffron and hid the same in his Palmer's staffe, which he had made hollow before of purpose and so he brought this root in this realme, with venture of his life, for if he had been taken, by the law of the country from whence it came [thought to be Tripoli] he died for the fact.

Saffron was used first and foremost as a dye, but medicinal properties were attributed to it, as a cure for jaundice, seasickness, even plague. The soils and climate of Walden proved ideal for saffron cultivation, and the town rapidly became the focus for an abundant harvest. The growers, known as 'crokers', had to fence the saffron gardens that were established on the slopes around the town to keep out pigs and other animals. William Harrison, rector of the nearby village of Radwinter (1571-1593), has left a most romantic account of saffron cultivation in his detailed *Description of England* (1577). Planting the crocus bulbs took place in July on heavily manured soil. 'Warm dark nightes, sweet dews, fat grounds and misty mornings' all helped to produce a good harvest in late September. The crokers were up early, as picking had to be completed by 11 a.m., before the blooms wilted. All the courtyards and alleys of the town would be heaped with discarded blue petals, as only the stigma (or chives) were kept, and 30,000 were needed to produce a single pound of dried saffron.

Tudor Walden

Walden's prosperity and influence reached a peak during the Tudor period, but at the end of the 15th century local trade increasingly suffered from manorial rights of toll, which were in the hands of the monarchy. Excessive tolls, such as a farthing on every quarter of malt brewed and a farthing for every shop window opened on a market day, drove traders to patronise the rival market at Newport.

After Henry VIII came to the throne several leading townspeople including John Leche, the vicar of Walden; his sister a wealthy London widow, Dame Joan Bradbury; and her son, James Bodley, together with William Bird and others, failed when they petitioned the king, offering to redeem the tolls for a substantial sum. They determined to establish a new religious guild, to which the king could grant the tolls and other manorial rights. It would operate like a town corporation, but be based on the chantry already envisaged by Katherine Semar, a wealthy widow of the town. The king granted a licence permitting the establishment of the Holy Trinity Guild. The guild met in a room over the south porch of the church, a custom continued by the later Corporation, who chose the mayor there each year until the 19th century. This ceremony is remembered in the annual churching of the mayor, which still continues.

One of the main achievements of the new guild was the establishment of the town's Grammar School. Earlier attempts had been foiled by the abbot of Walden, who jealously guarded the monks' monopoly of education. Inspired by her brother John Leche, Dame Joan Bradbury applied for a charter to establish the school. Although the charter was granted in 1525, the school had started four years earlier in a small house on the corner of Castle Street and Vicar Lane. It soon acquired new premises in Castle Street at Walsingham House, eventually moving to a new building in Ashdon Road in 1881. The Grammar School continued there until the 1940s, when it was closed and replaced by a new Secondary Modern School.

One of the pupils of the Grammar School in the 16th century was Sir Thomas Smith, who eventually rose to become Secretary of State to King Edward VI. Smith had encouraged the re-introduction of the saffron industry to the town, at a time when it was failing. When Henry VIII's attempts to confiscate the wealth of the chantries in 1547 threatened the continuation of the guilds which supported the almshouses and the Grammar School and were based on chantries, Smith and his family purchased the confiscated property for £600, and secured a royal charter establishing a new Corporation to administer both school and almshouses.

6 Sir Thomas Smith, 1512-1577. Born in Saffron Walden, he rose to be Secretary of State to Edward VI.

After Smith's death in 1577 his work, *De Republica Anglorum*, was published, the first systematic exposition of the supremacy of Parliament.

Walden's best known Elizabethan was without doubt the poet Gabriel Harvey, son of a local rope-maker. Harvey was immortalised in Spenser's *Shepherd's Calendar* as the character 'Hobbinol', and was the subject of a series of literary attacks by his contemporary and rival Thomas Nashe. Nashe directed several biting poetical satires at Harvey, including *Have With You to Saffron Walden*. The enmity Nashe felt for Harvey stemmed from the time when Nashe was asked by the monarchy to discover the identity of the author of the Marprelate tracts, a series of scurrilous attacks on the church and court, written by the self-styled *Martin Mar-prelate*. Nashe suspected that Harvey was the author, but couldn't prove it. (We now know that this was because Harvey was almost certainly not the author.) Harvey, who spent the last years of his life in Walden, was said to lack a sense of humour, but provoked it in others. His most lasting accomplishment was the development of the Harvey apple.

In spite of the town's prosperity, built on wool and saffron, the 16th century was traumatic. As well as the dispossession of the abbey in 1537, and the 'stripping of the altars' in 1553, the town was the muster point for the East Anglian gentry, prior to their bloody suppression of Kett's Norfolk rebellion in 1549. There was the 'Great Flood of Walden' which occurred at 6 a.m. on Michaelmas Day 1555, and four years later in 1559 the town was hit by a serious outbreak of plague. There was a second major epidemic in 1597, although the town avoided the worst of the 17th-century outbreaks, even when nearby villages such as Little Chesterford suffered badly in 1625 and 1638.

The Church

The original location of Walden's first church would have been close to the Anglo-Saxon burial ground in Abbey Lane. Christian burials were uncovered there during 19th-century excavations, and it must have been this wooden church which was given, with its property, to Walden Priory by Geoffrey de Mandeville (II). At some time a new stone-built church was erected near the castle on Bury Hill. The consecration of a new church at the Festival of St Mark in 1258 is recorded in the chronicles of Walden Abbey.

Nearly all of the present church dates from the 15th-century rebuilding, its predecessor apparently damaged in the great storm in 1445, which was noted by John Stowe: 'On Candlemas Even great weathering of wind, hayle, snow, rayne, thunders with lightning, whereby the Church of Walden in Essex and divers others were sore shaken'.

Twenty-five years later in 1470 work began on a new church, on such a scale that it took over fifty years to complete. Much of the later work was carried out under the supervision of John Wastell, the master mason responsible for the central tower at Canterbury Cathedral, the rebuilding of Great St Mary's, Cambridge, and the construction of King's College Chapel. Many of the carpenters employed on the chapel helped with the construction of Walden Church, while they were in the area selecting and transporting timber from abbey lands to Cambridge for King's College Chapel. It appears that while they were in the town they also constructed some of the rich timber-framed buildings that characterise the town, such as St Aylotts, and the building in Myddylton Place currently used as a youth hostel.

The richly decorated church was barely completed before it was plundered in 1553 by a Royal Commission sent to document and confiscate the wealth of local churches. Virtually everything was stripped from the church, and sold, apart from a cope, a chalice and patten, a lectern, and a cover for the communion table. The confiscated items were sold for £85, which was used for the relief of the poor and the maintenance of the school.

A lantern spire, supposedly designed by the lighthouse builder Henry Winstanley, was added to the church in the late 17th century. It survived until the 19th century, in spite of a severe storm in 1769 which badly damaged the building, and accelerated the deterioration of the fabric, so that by 1790 the church was forced to close for a short time. The church was renovated over the next forty years, and in 1832 a soaring perpendicular spire designed by Thomas Rickman was built to replace Winstanley's original.

The Civil War and the Birth of Democracy

Seventeenth-century Walden was not the prosperous community of the Elizabethan period. The population in 1666 was only 980 compared with 1,350 in 1524, a fall of 30 per cent. Hearth tax returns for the period suggest that 15 per cent of the population was too poor to pay the tax, and that some 13 per cent of the houses in the town stood empty. A small proportion of the population (about 6 per cent) owned 47 per cent of the town's taxable wealth—with a single family owning 7 per cent. Gold Street was the poorest part of the town. The decrease in population and the number of empty properties may reflect the decline in importance of saffron cultivation, and possibly the effects of plague and civil war—but this is only conjecture.

Saffron Walden was not immune to the general discontent of the period. In 1641 people in Newport pulled down the enclosure fences that had been put around the common land, and in the village of Radwinter an unpopular parson, Nicholas Drake, was ejected from his church by the congregation. When Drake erected a new screen in the church which contained carved figures of cherubim, local people urged soldiers to break down the figures, which were then carried to Saffron Walden and burnt in the Market Place.

During the Civil War, soldiers were frequently in the town, and in 1647 General Fairfax made the town the headquarters of the New Model Army. The army was in dispute with Parliament over arrears of pay. Parliament, which felt threatened by the radicalised soldiery, wanted to send the army to Ireland, but the troops were reluctant to go. Petitions began circulating amongst the rank and file and found support from the officers, much to Parliament's alarm. Parliament dispatched several commissioners to Walden to meet with officers in the church and persuade the soldiers to volunteer for Ireland.

The soldiers were increasingly coming under the influence of the democratic ideas of the Levellers, and formed a soldiers' council with elected representatives from each regiment. These representatives were called Agitators, and one of their first demands was that the officers should be elected by the ranks. The Agitators removed unsympathetic officers from their posts, established a clandestine press, and set up a secret network linking the army with the Leveller leaders in London. Messages were often written in code.

Parliament was alarmed by the increasing militancy of the army, and sent Cromwell to Saffron Walden to negotiate. On 3 May, the night that Cromwell arrived in the town, rumours of a rising against the army were circulating, and soldiers mounted an all-night guard on the streets with their swords drawn. The rumoured insurrection never occurred but the next day another clandestine pamphlet appeared, outlining an Agitator plan to control the army. Cromwell and his fellow commissioners summoned a meeting in the church, where they met with representatives of the common soldiers. The debates, which were acrimonious at times, ranged across the army's grievances, and raised all the issues of democracy and Ireland, arrears of pay, indemnity, and compensation, which were later raised in the better known Putney Debates after the army had marched on London.

Interestingly, the chairman of the Committee of Agitators was a local man, Sir John Reynolds, of Castle Camps, the third son of Sir James Reynolds who was head of the Essex Trained Bands. John Reynolds was educated as a lawyer, but joined the Parliamentary Army and played a distinguished part in the Parliamentary campaigns of the first Civil War. He took a leading part in organising opposition to the proposed disbanding of the army, and personally contributed to the Walden debates. Often referred to as one of Cromwell's 'favourites', he commanded one of the most radical regiments, and was one of the Parliamentary officers in charge of King Charles at Hurst Castle in December 1648.

There was little fighting in the area, except during the Siege of Colchester in 1648, when royalists, determined to break the siege, by drawing the army away from Colchester, established a rendezvous at the nearby village of Linton. Up to 500 men, both horse and foot, drawn from Saffron Walden, Bishops Stortford, and some of the nearby Suffolk and Cambridgeshire villages, gathered under the leadership of Captain Appleyard of Dullingham, and Colonel Mushame, a Scotsman with a wooden leg. They hoped to assemble 5,000 men within three days, but Fairfax was determined to crush the rising, and sent out a force from his army at Colchester. They attacked the royalists on 19 June, killing many, taking many more prisoner, and breaking the insurrection.

Religious Persecution and the Growth of Nonconformity
Walden nonconformity can be traced back to the teachings of John Bradford in Walden Church. Bradford, a chaplain to King Edward VI, refused to submit to Catholicism on the accession to the throne of Edward's sister Mary, and was burnt at the stake at Smithfield in 1555. From his prison he wrote a letter to his followers in Walden:

> Waver not in Christ's religion taught you and set forth in King Edwardes daies. Never shal the enemies be able to burne it, to prison it and keep it in bondes. Us they may prison, they may bind and burne ... but our cause ... they shal never be able to vanquish and put away.

The authorities felt so threatened by the number of Bradford's followers in the town that they sent John Newman, a travelling preacher from Kent, who had been arrested in the south of Essex, to be burnt in Walden as an example.

In the middle of the 17th century, when the Civil War had broken the religious monopoly of the state, a small group of Quakers began meeting in Walden. The initial response of the local magistrates was one of persecution. In 1656 one Quaker member was imprisoned, and another placed in the stocks in 1659. Quakers were heavily fined for meeting openly, as in 1669 when: 'For a meeting held at John Churchman's house, Wendon, he had goods taken worth £13 6s. 6d., Mathew Day of Newport £23 5s. 0d., Anthony Pennistone of Saffron Walden, £8 12s. 0d.'

In 1676 a cottage in Cucking Stool End Street (now High Street) was bought from Mathew Day for £20, and a back room, previously used for weaving, became the first Friends' Meeting House in the town. Magistrates remained determined to break the Quakers and ordered that the door to their Meeting House be nailed up. Undeterred, the Quakers

> held their Assembly in the street, whither the magistrates came, and tendered the Oath of Allegiance to Robert Flack and Richard Mansfield of Ashdon, and Thomas Trigg of Littlebury, and for refusing to take it, sent them to prison.

The Quakers were prepared to make a declaration of allegiance, but had religious objections to taking oaths. Nailing the door up twice cost the Corporation 4d. The Quakers were not easily deterred and, as their meetings grew, so they enlarged their premises by buying up the adjacent cottages.

Quakers were not the only nonconformists, and when Rev. Jonathan Paine, a preacher who had been evicted from Bishop's Stortford church for refusing to accept the Act of Uniformity, came to the area in 1665 he quickly attracted the descendants of John Bradford's followers. After the Toleration Act (1689) Paine and his congregation began worshipping regularly in a barn in Abbey Lane. Within a few years, these Independents had purchased and pulled down several tenements which stood on Frogs Orchard near the barn, and by 1694 had built their own chapel. Membership of the chapel was comprised of Baptists and Independents, but in 1773 an enthusiastic new Baptist minister at the chapel, Rev. Joseph Gwennap, attracted new members and the Baptists soon outnumbered the Independents. After a dispute about ownership of the chapel, Gwennap and his followers broke away, at first holding their meetings in Elizabeth Fuller's barn in Myddylton Place until they built their own chapel in Bailey's Lane (now Audley Road). At various times at least two other Baptist churches existed in the town. A congregation of Particular Baptists established a Meeting House near Cates Corner in 1711, and a second breakaway faction from the Abbey Lane Congregational Chapel founded a strict Baptist Chapel in London Road in 1819.

Methodism also had a stormy beginning in Walden when two women preachers settled in the town in 1823. Charlotte Berger and her friend Mrs. Webster had been visiting the town and preaching in a converted Castle Street barn for two years, before taking up residence next door. Prejudice against women preachers soon led to attacks on their home, and the interruption of their services by drunks and unruly youths. The women appealed to the magistrates, who jailed two of the men and warned the others.

The strength of the Nonconformist religions in Walden became significant after the Municipal Corporations Act of 1835, which widened the franchise and removed the bar on Nonconformists holding public positions. In elections held that year nine of the 16 elected members were Nonconformists, four Quakers and five from the Abbey Lane Congregational Chapel. These men, like the first nonconformist mayor, John Player, were to create a new identity for Saffron Walden.

The late 18th century was marked by serious rural unrest. East Anglia was shaken by bread riots, and Saffron Walden was no exception. Successive poor harvests resulted in a dramatic increase in the price of corn. Local authorities tried to stabilise the price, and arranged for the distribution of relief supplies, but matters came to a head in July 1795 when a crowd drinking in the yard at the *Greyhound* (now the *Saffron Walden Weekly News* office) stormed the loft and carried off the corn. Numbers grew, and the crowd made their headquarters at the *White Horse*, sending out parties of men to requisition food at less than the market price, which they distributed freely. For a few hours the town was in the hands of the rioters, until the militia arrived from Chelmsford, and arrested the organisers, including a local cooper, Samuel Porter. Those arrested were charged with attacking various tradesmen and compelling them to sell food. Porter was condemned to 'pay a fine of £50 and be imprisoned in the common gaol one year and until he pay the said fine'. Other rioters received prison sentences of three to six months.

Social upheaval continued well into the 19th century, with disturbances associated with 'Captain Swing' in many local villages. In Saffron Walden itself, the workhouse, which was located at the southern end of Cucking Stool End Street (now High Street), was burnt down just before Christmas 1835; its occupants danced around the fire, and prevented the firemen from putting out the flames. A grim new purpose-built workhouse was constructed in Radwinter Road to replace it.

Saffron Walden was transformed in the 19th century. Buildings like the old Woolstaplers' Hall, which had dominated the Market Place and once provided a focus for the social life of the town, were pulled down. New buildings, like the Corn Exchange, were built, and new institutions such as the Museum and the Literary and Scientific Institute (now the Library) were formed. Nonconformists like John Player and George Stacey Gibson were instrumental in this transformation. Player was a prime mover in the formation of both the Museum and the Institute, and was responsible for setting up allotments in the town—the first in the country. Gibson, a Quaker landowner, with extensive interests in malting, brewing, and banking, brought the railway to Saffron Walden, and provided land and money to set up the Friends' School, the Teacher Training College, and the British Schools. Other members of the Gibson family provided the financial initiative for the hospital, which was built by public subscription; the gasworks and the new water company.

Many of the new Victorian buildings were designed by architects of note: the Corn Exchange (Tress), the Hospital (Beck), the Friends' School, the Training College, and the new front to the Town Hall (Burgess). Gibson's bank, which later became a constituent part of Barclays, erected a magnificent red-brick building, designed by Eden Nesfield, in the Market Place.

The new buildings and the new institutions they housed shaped the town and its character right through until the early 1960s. Even now the Museum, Library and Town Hall continue to provide a focus for the cultural life of Saffron Walden. Unfortunately the process of contraction and closure, which began in the 1960s with the closing of the railway station, still continues, with the threat to close the hospital and magistrates courts. The greatest challenge lies ahead as technological change and administrative centralisation alter our world: can the people of Saffron Walden retain the identity of the community that has taken over 2,000 years to evolve?

Buildings and Monuments

7 The Woolstaplers' Hall shortly before it was demolished in 1848 to make way for the Corn Exchange. Originally built sometime between 1470 and 1510, it was at one time part of the *Iron Crown Inn*. Long before demolition it had been sub-divided into dwellings, so that only the magnificent carved hammer-beams remained visible.

8 The Corn Exchange, 1849. Designed by Richard Tress in what Pevsner describes as a 'jolly and tasteless Italian style' it was built by Erswells, of Saffron Walden, on the site of the old Woolstaplers' Hall. Trading in corn took place from small dealing desks inside. Nearly demolished when corn trading ceased, it was converted into the Library and Arts Centre which opened in 1975.

9 The Town Hall was built in 1761 to replace the Guild Hall. Guy Maynard writes that someone was once tied to the iron gates and whipped. The present mock Tudor front was added in 1879. Boardman's of Bishop's Stortford purchased Youngman's printing and bookselling business when he became a professional artist.

10 Audley End mansion depicted in the late 17th century by Henry Winstanley. Built in 1603 on the site of the abbey, at a cost of over £200,000, it originally consisted of an inner court, 205 feet square on the inside, with open arcades on two sides, a smaller central court, the eastern side of which formed a gallery 226 feet long. Its upkeep proved too expensive and most of the principal court was demolished under the direction of Sir John Vanbrugh, and the gallery was removed in 1708.

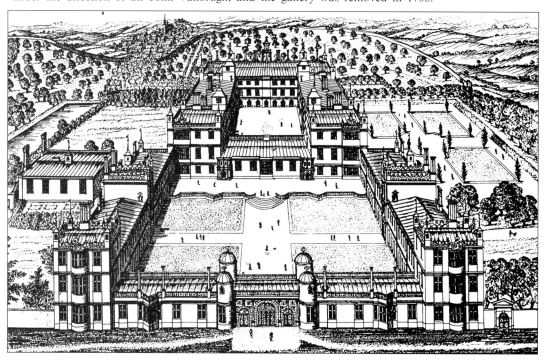

11 Audley End mansion. The building which remains is only a small part of the original Jacobean palace. The Tudor building on the left, known as 'The Stables', was in fact the Walden Abbey hostel, and predates the mansion.

12 Audley End mansion in the early 19th century.

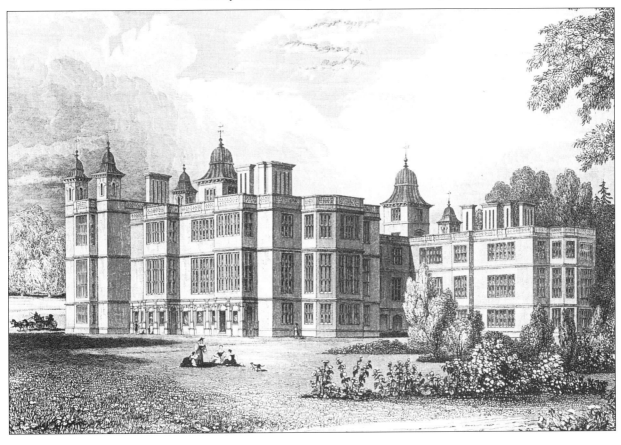

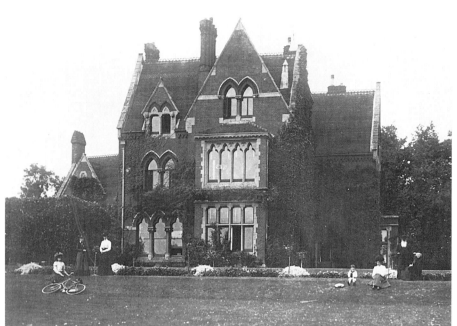

13 The Vineyard, Windmill Hill, designed by the Quaker architect William Beck for the Tuke family of Quaker bankers. Beck also designed the London Road Hospital. The Vineyard got its name from its proximity to the site of the Walden Abbey vineyard.

14 The Vineyard, interior, 1908.

15 Walden Place, August 1915, was used as a British Red Cross Hospital during the First World War. Walden Place is built on Hogg's Green, one of the oldest parts of the town. Until its conversion to sheltered accommodation for the elderly it was the home of the de Paula family.

16 Walden Lodge, Audley End Park. Built in 1814 and possibly designed by Rickman, Walden Lodge was enlarged in the 1970s.

17 Icehouse Lodge, Audley End Park. The lodge was designed by Henry Harrison and built between 1825 and 1827. The gate arch was designed by Thomas Rickman.

18 Hill House, High Street, from the garden, *c*.1860. *From left to right*: Pitstow, Edith Mennell, Mary Gibson, Elizabeth Gibson, Francis Gibson, and F. Brown. Note the cap of the High Street/Gold Street maltings on the far right. *See also* illustrations 138 and 145.

19 The drinking fountain was designed by John Bentley, the architect of Westminster Cathedral. Exhibited at the Imperial Exhibition of 1862, it was purchased by the Gibson family and presented to the town, to commemorate the marriage of the Prince of Wales (later Edward VII). The carved panels depict Moses in scenes from the Old Testament.

20 High Street, 1948. Thirty feet high, the War Memorial is built of Portland stone. Carved wreaths decorate four of its eight sides. A wreath of wild rose surrounding a shield with St George in relief faces north; a wreath of oak surrounding the Essex arms faces south; a wreath of saffron crocus with shield depicting the town arms faces west; and a wreath enclosing the old town seal, a lion rampant and fleur-de-lys in relief faces east. *See also* illustrations 134 and 135.

21 Gibson Free Dwellings, Abbey Lane, *c*.1910. Built by the Gibson family between 1840 and 1850 to house retired employees, they were given to the Almshouse trustees in 1950, but subsequently sold.

22 Almshouses. These buildings were built on Almshouse meadow to replace the original medieval almshouses and were completed in 1834. The doors in the front of the building have been blocked up and replaced by windows. *See also* illustrations 112 and 118.

23 The Water Tower, Debden Road, *c*.1915. Erected near the Friends' School, by the Borough, the foundation stone was laid by the Mayor, J.P. Atkinson, M.D., J.P., on 9 May 1913. Designed by the Borough Surveyor, A.H. Forbes, it was built by the local builders, Custersons, who used 32,500 bricks. It was replaced by a new tower on the Thaxted Road in 1966.

24 High Street, *c*.1830. This part of High Street was known as Cucking Stool End Street, taking its name from the pond formed by blocking a section of the Battle Ditches near Margaret Way. The building on the right was a maltings, which was demolished in the 1970s. Next to the maltings is Powell's Corner, now Gold Street.

25 Gold Street, *c*.1910. Once one of the poorest streets in Walden, it also housed many of the town's maltings. Most of the maltings have now been demolished, but some remain, converted into homes, their original purpose concealed behind 18th- and 19th-century façades.

26 Malting played a vital part in Walden's prosperity from the 14th century until the 19th century, when the industry was at its peak. At that time there were over thirty maltings in the town. These maltings were part of a large complex behind High Street, and were photographed shortly before demolition in 1958. Barnards Court has since been built on the site.

27　The *Axe and Compass*, Ashdon Road, with Charles Walls, blacksmith, *c*.1890.

28　Market Hill, looking down towards the *King's Arms* and the *Green Dragon*, *c*.1930. The *Green Dragon* became a saddler's shop in 1934, and the sign was used on a pub in Sewards End. It then became the Trustee Savings Bank in 1950. Bruce Munro's Estate Agency, which now occupies one of the buildings on the right, was the original office for Gibson's Bank.

29 Dolphin House, Gold Street, *c*.1935. The pargetted Dolphin sign was moved from the *Dolphin Inn* in Market Street when it was demolished in 1761 to make way for the new Town Hall.

30 The *Cross Keys*, High Street, is thought to date from the 14th century. This view was taken before the plasterwork was removed. The building was the *Bull's Head* in 1709, but 60 years later was a 'Baking Office', and by 1778 had taken over the name of the Cross Keys. The original *Cross Keys Inn* was located in Cross Street.

31 Renovation in 1920, when the plaster-work was removed, and new details added to the windows. Removal of the plaster shows clearly where an additional storey was added in the late 18th or early 19th century.

32 *Above*. The *Cross Keys* after renovation. Note Wright's Garage in High Street.

33 *Left*. The *Sun Inn*, with its decorated plaster-work, or pargetting, a feature that can be seen on many old buildings in the town, and in this instance depicts the mythical giants Gog and Magog. It is supposed to have been Fairfax's Headquarters during the English Civil War. 23 Church Street is where photographer William Frost Wilson had his photographic studio in 1906, and where tailor John Baynes Burton set up business in 1911, making livery for Lord Braybrooke. Burton was a volunteer fireman and received a long service medal. This photograph was taken about 1925.

34 *Right*. No. 23 Church Street in 1993, when the plaster was stripped from the front revealing the timber framing. Probably once part of the *Sun Inn* complex, the right half of the building was originally jettied like the left side before Victorian alterations. Some small 16th-century windows were uncovered.

35 The *Rose and Crown*, Market Place, *c.*1930. An election occurred during the construction of the railway in the 1860s. Both Liberals and Conservatives hired all the navvies they could find and plied them with drink. Fighting broke out around the boards displaying the state of the poll. The *Rose and Crown*, the Conservative HQ, was vigorously assailed with rotten eggs 'until the front wept yellow tears' and was stormed by the Liberals. Hand-to-hand combat was eventually stopped by the police.

36 The *Rose and Crown* public bar, Christmas 1947.

37 The *White Horse*, Market Street. It has been an inn with the same name since at least 1687. During the food riots of 1795 it was used as the headquarters of the rioters, who sent out groups of men to requisition food from the shops.

38 *The Greyhound*, High Street, June 1953. This is the inn where the Food Riots started in 1795, when Sam Porter and others seized the grain that was stored in the loft.

39 Dobson's Hairdresser's in King Street, 1906, now the Corner Cupboard. Traditionally, the timber-work on timber-framed houses in this part of Essex is left covered with plasterwork, but at the turn of the century a craze for exposing old timbers resulted in many fine old buildings losing their protective plaster.

40 King Street, 1930. It is difficult to believe that a narrow row of buildings, known as Middle Row, ran down the centre, with Guild Hall and Town Gaol standing at the Market Place end. Note the old *Hoops* public house on the right, and the *Rose and Crown* in Market Place at the far end of King Street.

41 Thaxted Road, *c*.1912. *The Gate* public house was the last building in the town on that side of the road.

42 Castle Street in 1950. On the evening of May Day Castle Street folk used to play a game called 'Pig in the gutter'. Adorned with flowers they joined hands, formed a long line, and led by 'Royal Moll' rushed through the streets whooping like Indians. Unsuspecting passers-by caught up in the throng either had to join in or pay a 'toll'.

Trade and Commerce

43 The Market Place, *c.*1820. The dilapidated market cross had been demolished in 1818, and the whipping post moved to Castle Street. Winstanley's lantern spire on the church was replaced in 1832. The weighbridge in front of the town malt mill is clearly depicted.

44 The Market Place, 1951. The market moved to Walden from Newport in 1141. Originally sited inside the castle bailey, in the general area of what is currently the Close Garden, in High Street, it was moved in the 13th century to make way for the construction of High Street, and (probably) the church which was built at about that time.

45 Burningham's hairdressers, Market Place. Miss Mary Walls and Gilbert Foan. The shop is now part of the NatWest Bank.

46 Pope's, Market Place, *c*.1930. Tom Wright and Freda Hobbs in the doorway. The shop now sold toys as well as cutting hair. In the 1950s and early 1960s it was called Startup's.

47 Wabon's in King Street, 1908. This view was taken shortly after a fire broke out at Woodward's auctioneers, immediately across the road from Wabon's. The fire was hot enough to blister and scorch the paint on the shutters.

48 Wabon's later became Barrett's sweet shop, then Molly's Candy Store. It is now part of the *Cross Keys* public house.

49 *Above*. King Street, looking towards High Street. The building on the left with the regency window is now Stephen Williams' opticians, and the building on the right is Occasions card shop.

50 *Left*. The Post Office and shops built in King Street in 1890 by Whiffen and Sons, local builders. The shop on the right, 8 King Street, now Radio Rentals, is where Henry Day had his watch, clock and jewellery business until 1911, when he was succeeded by Arthur Francis James. W.H. Smith's now occupies the old post office.

51 *Opposite, above left*. A. James (Jewellers) Ltd., 41 King Street, *c*.1911. Established in 1863 at 8 King Street by William Rickman Jeffery. In 1871 Jeffery was succeeded by John James. When James died in 1883 his son-in-law Henry William Day continued the business until his retirement in 1911. He handed over to Arthur Francis James (John's son), who moved the premises to 41 King Street, where he continued until his death in 1932. In 1958 the business moved to 4 King Street, where the managing director is Brian Newman.

52 *Opposite, above right*. Hardwicks, fishmongers, King Street, *c*.1928-36. George Clarke was manager there for 44 years.

53 *Right*. The January sales at Booth's in King Street, 1950.

54 The studio of photographer J.E. Galley, in London Road, decorated for the Coronation, 1911. Galley was one of the town's most prolific photographers. Edgar's the dentists is now in this building.

55 David Miller's bakery, London Road, c.1914. Note the old post office sign above the shop. The building is now used as a hairdresser's.

56 High Street, *c.*1895. The building on the right was Hughes' coach-building business, now Walden motors. The brick building next to it was the *Clifton Hotel.*

57 The Saffron Walden Co-operative Society, High Street, 1906. Walden's first Co-op opened in Castle Street in 1902. The High Street shop opened in 1905 and sold groceries, hardware, drapery, outfitting and shoes.

58 Charles Start, Ted Stock and William Clarke at work in the Co-op bakery. The first Co-op bakery was situated in Ashdon Road, but this new bakehouse was built in 1912 at the rear of the High Street shop. The bakery was later used as the Labour Hall but is now used by Wilbur's Gym.

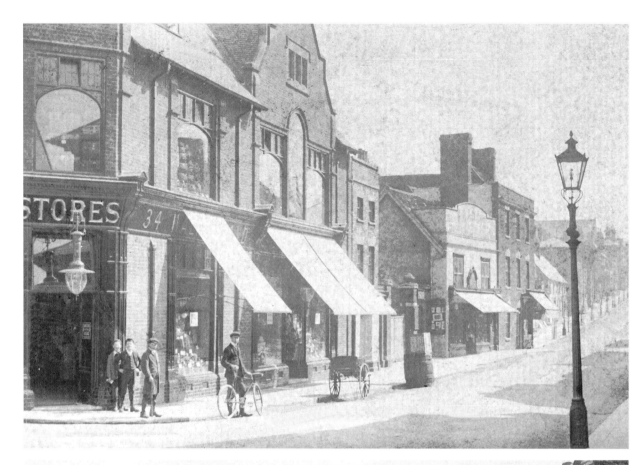

59 *Left*. Walker's Stores, High Street, 1912.

60 *Below left*. High Street, looking south, Cro's Market Stores, Bunting's florist and fruit shop and Taylor's bakery shown on the right.

61 *Right*. Herbert Burton and family outside 6 High Street, *c*.1930. He was a third generation saddler in a business started in 1782. *Left to right*: Dorothy Cole, Nellie Cliff, Alice Burton (née Wyatt), Daisy Burton, Herbert Burton. (Herbert and Alice Burton were great-grandparents of co-author Howard Newman.) George Stacey Gibson was born in this house.

62 *Below*. Bridge End, looking north, *c*.1920. The shop on the right was where Tom Goddard started his butcher's business, before moving to Church Street. His sausage recipe is legendary in the town and is still used by Grayson and Start who bought the recipe when Goddard's closed.

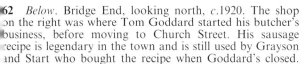

63 Jennings Estate Agents in Cross Street, *c.*1912. Ernest Jennings is in the doorway. When Slocombe (the auctioneer mentioned on the window) died, the business was run by his wife until it was purchased by Ernest Jennings for £25 in 1906.

64 Castle Street looking west, *c.*1911. A.C. Marsh the baker stands outside his shop.

65 Isaac Marking's butcher's shop, at the corner of Church Street and Museum Street, *c.*1920. *Left to right*: George Watson, Bert Shepherd, Isaac Marking. Marking was a fireman, and was always first to arrive at the fire station after the alarm bell rang. He died in 1944.

66 Cooper's music shop at the corner of Audley
Road and Fairycroft Road.

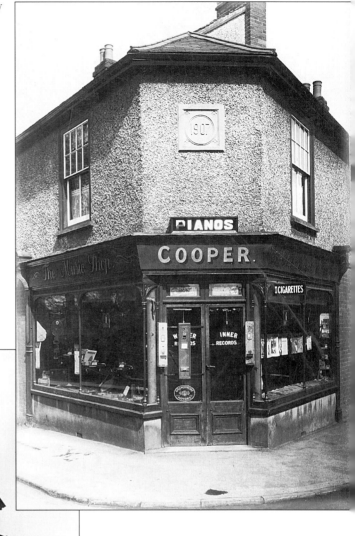

67 Market Row, 1954. The town's telephone
exchange was once situated in the building on the
left.

Transport and Roads

68 Joseph Wright at his cycle shop, 25 High Street, c.1897. Realising the possibilities of the motor car, Wright pioneered the motor trade in the town until his retirement in 1919. He died in 1931 aged 69. After Wright moved across the road, the shop was for many years the Radio Supply Stores, but is currently the Drop-In Centre, for young people.

69 Wright's business expanded across the road to 26 High Street. Later demolished to become Woolworth's, Wright's cycle shop became a car showroom in 1912. The car on the left is Wright's own 18-22 horse power Darracq Limousine. The car on the right is an 8-10 horse power Phoenix 2-seater belonging to Walter Thompson of the Grammar School. Petrol at this time was only available from Robson and Sons' premises in Station Road and King Street or from Wright's Garage.

70 Frank Wright, with a 12-14 horse power UNIC owned by Mrs. Annie Cooper of White Lodge, Newport, outside London Road Hospital, 1910.

71 Hughes and Sons, carriage builders, High Street, *c*.1907. Now Walden Motors and Russell Green's Undertakers. The next building down the hill was the *Clifton Hotel*, now the Pine Shop.

72 The George Street showroom of coach builders Wedd and Son, which was later used to display agricultural equipment for Choppen's, but is now a small row of shops.

73 Raynham's Garage, High Street, 1920, before the building of the showroom in 1921. Although it was owned by the Gibson family in the early part of the 19th century, the building was already the 'common Brewhouse' in a survey in 1758.

74 Raynham's Garage after the construction of the showroom in 1921. It was built by local engineer Rex Osborne, whose family owned a specialised motor vehicle body-building work-shop in the town.

75 Raynham's Garage in 1948. The garage closed in 1998, and Raynham's business was transferred to Newport. The brewery building was converted into houses, but the glass showroom, and some internal 14th-century timber-framing were demolished.

76 Market Street was once known as Market Bridge Street, as there was a bridge over the Slade or King's Ditch at this point. Just past the sweet shop (now the Golden Butterfly), where the Saffron Walden Herts and Essex Building Society now stands is the site of the old cattle market. Note the old market bell on the market shed. The old maltings in the corner of the Market Place were demolished to make way for Emson Close in the 1960s.

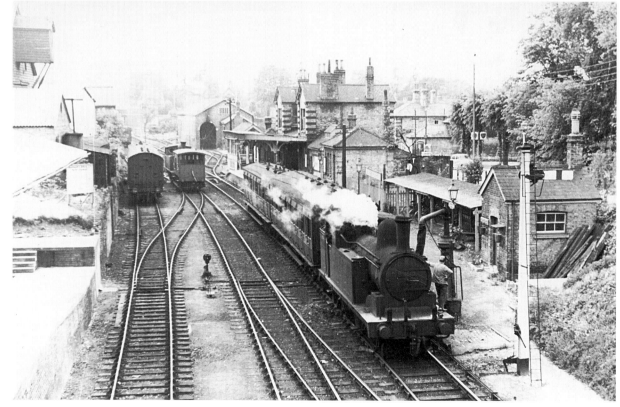

77 *Left*. Saffron Walden railway station, 1905. Quakers, Wyatt George Gibson and George Stacey Gibson together with John Robson, James Stanley and Joshua Clarke set up the Saffron Walden Railway Company in 1861 to bring a branch-line to the town. The first train on the line ran on 23 November 1865.

78 *Below left*. Saffron Walden railway station, 1955. The Audley End-Saffron Walden railway line opened in November 1865, and was extended to Bartlow to connect with the Shelford-Marks Tey line in 1866. The station was closed during the Beeching cuts in 1964.

79 *Below*. Audley End railway station, 1909, looking towards London from the platform for Cambridge.

80 *Above*. Williams' Livery Stables, Freshwell Street, 1905. Mounted left to right: Bill Marking, Frank Port, Tom Phillips, Richard Atkinson Williams, H. Hockley. The fire brigade relied on Williams' horses to pull the engine, so when there was a fire they had to be rushed to the fire station.

81 *Below*. New Pond, Freshwell Street. The delivery trap belonged to F.J. Taylor, a High Street baker. The pond was reshaped after the First World War when a road was built linking Freshwell Street with Park Lane, and again when the car park was built at Swan Meadow. Construction of the car park was one of the most bitterly fought local planning disputes, and resulted in two public inquiries.

82 *Above right*. Delivery cart for Nunn and Sons in Radwinter Road, 1906. Nunn's was a general ironmongers, china and glass merchants in Market Row.

83 *Below right*. Flour delivery at Fitch's café and bakery at the top of High Street. The steam-powered delivery engine came from J.H. King's mill at Great Chesterford, 1912.

84 Frederick White with Co-op van. He lost a leg in the First World War and eventually became a basket maker in Barnard's Yard.

85 Conservative women's visit to the Houses of Parliament; departure from the Market Place, July 1928.

Schools and Services

86 Friends' School, Saffron Walden, *c.*1904. A Quaker boarding school, the Friends' School moved to Saffron Walden from Croydon in 1879. The school, designed by Edward Burgess, was built on land given by George Stacey Gibson.

87 The interior of the chemistry labs, Friends' School in 1905.

THE FRIENDS' SCHOOL, SAFFRON WALDEN. CHEMICAL LABORATORY.

88 The dining hall, Friends' School in 1905.

89 The swimming pool, Friends' School in 1905.

90 The gymnasium, Friends' School n 1905.

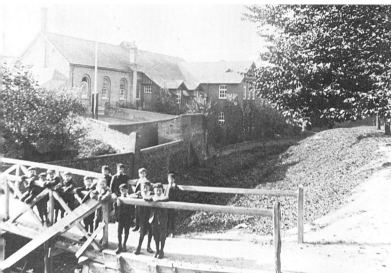

91 Wooden bridge across the Slade. It was replaced by a metal bridge in 1905. A surplus from Edward VII's Coronation Fund was used to finance the new bridge which cost £131. The Boys' British School, which was built in 1838, can be seen in the background. Within a year of opening there were 106 children on the register, although parents had to pay 2d. a week for each boy who went to the school.

92 The opening of the new metal bridge across the Slade. Note the washing on lines at the top of the Common put there by Castle Street residents who lacked anywhere else to dry their laundry.

93 *Above.* Grammar School Ashdon Road. Built in 1881, i was used as headquarters of th 65th Fighter wing of the Unite States Army Air Force durin the Second World War. Afte the war it was used as a hoste for student teachers. Mor recently it has been the home o the Dame Bradbury School which was started after the wa in Nissen huts in the schoo grounds, and now has th benefit of the Grammar Schoo charity.

94 *Left.* The first pupils arriv in the main entrance of the ne Secondary Modern School o the first day of lessons, Januar 1951. Before the new buildin was ready lessons were held a Fairycroft.

95 The Secondary Modern School rapidly became known as the 'New School'. Washing hands in the foot-operated fountains was a novelty, 1951.

96 Student teachers playing tennis at the rear of the Training College, 1905. The Girls' British School, which was attached to the Training College, opened in 1902, and provided student teachers with opportunities for teaching practice. The buildings are now used by the Bell language school.

97 The Teacher Training College, *c*.1930. George Stacey Gibson gave the ground and £10,000 for the building, which was designed by Edward Burgess. The college opened in 1884 and closed in 1978. Teaching was based on the popular and progressive Froebel method.

98 A visiting group of malnourished school children from Rotterdam arrives at Saffron Walden station to stay with local families in 1946. They were met at the station by Rev. Stephen Harris and Alderman and Mrs. Custerson, all members of the Abbey Lane Chapel. The Dutch teacher on the right was Conny van der Stoel.

99 Dancing lessons in the playground of St Mary's School, Castle Street, 1952.

100 The retirement of Joseph Elsden, Headmaster of the Boys' British School, in 1965. Former pupils Ted Brewer, John Stubbs and Mr. Tredgett are in the front row of the audience. Mr. Elsden is standing on the right of the photograph.

101 Saffron Walden Hospital, 1908. Designed by William Beck, and built on land given by Lord Braybrooke, it cost £5,504 to build; £600 for furniture and a further £100 to equip the dispensary. Costs were met by a bequest of £5,000 from Wyatt George Gibson in 1862, and by public subscription. Opened in 1866, it became the offices of Uttlesford District Council in 1990.

102 Saffron Walden Fire Brigade, *c.*1911. *Back row*, *left to right*: Julius Green; ?; ? Fred J. Pateman; John Baynes Burton; Arthur Day; Albert Housden; *front*, *left to right*: John Gilling; ?; Harold Dix (boy); Chief Officer Andrew R. Dix; A.H. Forbes, Borough Surveyor; Foreman George Wyatt (seated); Isaac Marking; H. Burton; C.W. Land (reporter, *Saffron Walden Weekly News*).

103 Walden Fire Brigade, 1931. The History of Walden's fire brigade can be traced back to 1655 when the sexton was paid 2s. 6d. for 'twice filling and emptying the engin [*sic*], and for making three covers'. The modern brigade was established in 1865 with 16 volunteers. *Left to right* (*back row*): Engineer J.A. Choppen; Herbert Day; Cliff Choppen; Dick Selves Jnr.; Frank Ketteridge. (*front row*): Chief Officer Clem Miller; Second Officer Arthur J. Dix; Foreman Herbert Wyatt; Hubert Bell; Teddy Worley; Dick Selves, Snr.

104 Fire at Hughes & Sons, High Street. From left to right: Isaac Marking, E.H. Crow, Andrew R. Dix, the Chief Fire Officer.

105 Aftermath of the fire at the old Highways Depot, Hill Street, now the fire station yard, *c*.1920.

106 A fire engine leaves the Hill Street fire station for another emergency call, *c.*1947.

107 The Literary and Scientific Institute, King Street, 1965. Founded in 1832 by Jabez and Francis Gibson, and John Player, trusteeship passed to Essex County Council Libraries in 1967 when it became known as the Town Library. It was a condition of the trust that the Institute's collection of some 20,000 volumes must remain in Saffron Walden. Housed in the same building that has been its home for nearly 150 years, the Town Library is the centrepiece of a busy Victorian Studies Centre, receiving over 3,000 enquiries each year.

Church and Religion

108 St Mary's Church before 1832. The lantern spire was designed by Henry Winstanley whose father was church-warden. Best known for his Eddystone lighthouse, Winstanley was paid £8 for painting and contriving the dial and motion of the church clock in 1678. Its complex mechanism combined old-fashioned orbs rising and setting like the sun and moon with tunes played by eight hammers on bells.

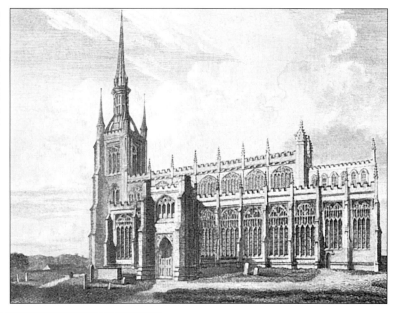

109 St Mary's Church after 1832. In 1832 a new spire designed by Thomas Rickman was added. The height of the spire from the weathercock to the ground is 193 feet. The clock in the tower was installed in 1823 at a cost of £240. At one time a representation of St George was painted on its face.

110 New bells on display on the steps of St Mary's Church, before rehanging, June 1914. Members of the Society of Change Ringers. *Left to right*: Charles Freeman; J.F. Penning; R.A. Strong; A.F. James; John Gilling (churchwarden); Rev. G.M. Benton (curate), representative from the bell foundry; Rev. J.J. Antrobus (vicar); Frederick Pitstow; Rev. G.F. Hart (curate); Harold Pitstow; Alfred Pitstow; Alfred Evenett; Walter Parrish. *Seated*: Frederick Pitstow Jr.; Leonard Pitstow; George Sparrow.

111 St Aylotts, *c.*1835. Built in 1500 for John Sabysforth, Abbot of Walden, on the site of an earlier chapel dedicated to St Aylott. According to a manuscript 'Lives of the Saints' (pre-1634), St Aylott 'was martered at a place bearing his name in Essex 2 miles from Walden, where there was a Chappell dedicated to him and where there hathe bene many myracles shewn by him'.

112 The chapel on the north front of the almshouses built in *c.*1400 by the Guild of Our Lady of Pity. Situated in Daniels Lane (later called Almshouse Lane, but now Park Lane), the almshouses faced William Myddylton's mansion on Hoggs Green. In 1530 he complained of the 'lusty men' from the almshouses who called to solicit alms every morning. These buildings were demolished in 1782. *See also* illustrations 22 and 118.

113 Interior of the Catholic Church of Our Lady of Compassion. Local Catholics were persecuted in the late 16th and early 17th centuries. Jane Wiseman of Braddocks at Wimbish was 'the most notorious recusant of the county' and was sentenced to death by pressing for sheltering a priest. The sentence was retracted but she remained in prison for several years. The church was originally a barn in the gardens to the Close which belonged to Francis Gibson. Purchased by Father Charles Chase, a former Hussar who became a Catholic priest, it was opened for worship in 1906. The first permanent priest was appointed in 1910, the same year in which a convent school was opened in the Close.

114 The original Abbey Lane Chapel built in Frog's Orchard, Abbey Lane, in 1694.

115 Abbey Lane Chapel after rebuilding in 1811. The tomb of the first minister, Rev. Jonathan Paine, is built under the chapel and supports the building.

116 The interior of Abbey Lane Chapel. Critics mocked it as a theatre, and produced a satirical poster which was displayed around the town after the 1811 rebuilding. The organ was added in 1858, and new pews were installed in 1888, when the pulpit was lowered and enlarged. The clock, donated by ladies of the church, is original.

117 Congregational Chapel Hall, Abbey Lane, originally built as a schoolroom for the chapel Sunday School in 1861. On the left is Miss M.A. Walls, who owned the toyshop next to the town hall, and on the right Miss A. Edwards, Dame of the Almshouse. The tombstones were cleared from the burial ground in 1960-1.

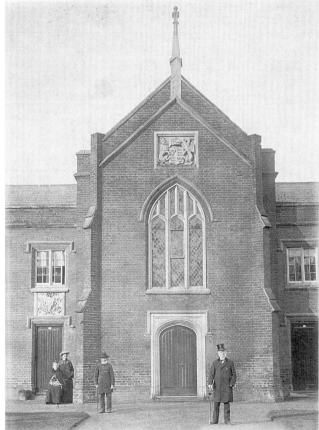

118 Almshouse Chapel, Abbey Lane, c.1900. The man on the right with the top hat was Thomas Wyatt of George Street, aged 70 years, who was elected to the Almshouses in 1894. He was the great-great-uncle of Olive Newman, wife of the current Almshouse master, Brian Newman. *See* illustrations 22 and 112.

119 Church Lads' Brigade, on the church steps with Rev. Philip Wright, 1942. Wright was a curate at Saffron Walden before becoming vicar at Littlebury. He wrote several books, including one about old agricultural machinery.

120   The chapel inside the Carmelite convent, 1970. The nuns' chapel was separated from the public one in the convent by a large arch completely filled with a large grille, through which the nuns witnessed the service without being seen. The convent was situated in Ashdon Road, at the top of the Common, and was founded by Miss Coates, and opened by Cardinal Bourne in 1928. The convent itself was demolished in 1974 and de Bohun Court and Fitzpiers now occupy the site.

121   Nuns at the Carmelite convent in 1970. The order was enclosed, and the nuns did not appear in public.

War and Remembrance

22 Last parade of 'I' Company, 3rd Cambridge Volunteer Battalion, Suffolk Regiment, Market Place, 1908. This was the last parade of the Volunteers before they were superseded by the Territorials. Note the town band at the back. The officer at the front is Capt. William Ackland.

123 *Left*. Departure of the Territorials for the front during the First World War. The Mayor, Frances Atkinson, with the beard, is seeing them off from the southern end of High Street, where the war memorial was later erected. The buildings behind were part of the local gaol in the late 18th and early 19th centuries.

124 *Below left*. A bi-plane which was forced to land for repairs during army manoeuvres, 16 September 1912. Landing first at Shire Hill, it then flew a short distance to a field behind Coe's Farm in Peaslands Road. Local children were given the day off school to go and see it.

125 *Below*. Soldiers wounded during the First World War arriving at Saffron Walden station, before being taken to the temporary hospital at Walden Place, October 1914.

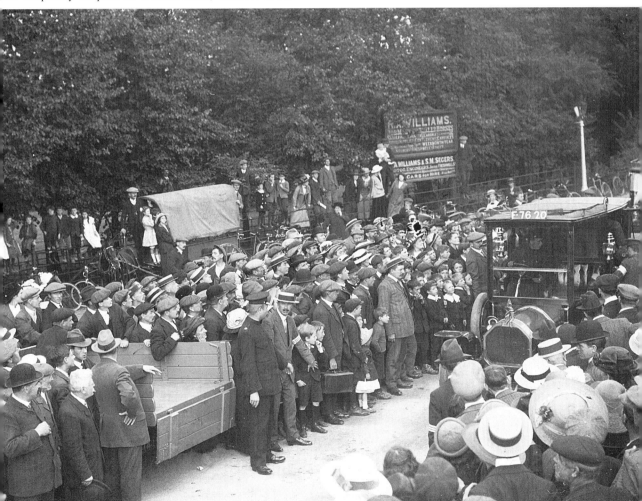

126 The Priory, Common Hill, Saffron Walden, with soldiers stationed in the town during the First World War. The Priory, which is built over one of the medieval ditches around the town, was used as a school for many years.

127 Wounded soldiers recovering at Saffron Walden Hospital, 1916. The London Road Hospital was opposite the home of a Quaker pacifist, Arthur Midgley. When the first wounded soldiers arrived back in Saffron Walden, Midgley was host to German visitors, and local people staged a large and rowdy demonstration outside his house.

128 Red Cross nurses with injured patients. The nursing staff included Sister Smith (top left), Mrs. Atkinson and Miss M. Clayden (front left), and Matron Winter (second row, centre).

129 Members of the London and Scottish Regiment who were stationed in the town during the First World War. Note the dog adopted as a mascot.

B.W.T.A. SOLDIERS' RECREATION ROOM.
FRIENDS' MEETING HOUSE, SAFFRON WALDEN, 1915.

130 Friends' Meeting House during the First World War, used by the British Women's Temperance Association as a recreation room for soldiers. The banner hanging from the gallery reads: 'Four good reasons for total abstinence. My head is clearer, My health is better, My heart is lighter, My pulse is heavier'.

131 Peace celebrations in 1919. The captured German field gun was put on display at the Museum, but was eventually melted down for scrap in the Second World War. The Roll of Honour commemorating local men killed in action was displayed in the church until 1995, when a new one was carved. The original is now in the Museum.

132   Dinner given in the Corn Exchange to members of the armed forces who had returned from the war, 19 July 1919.

133 *Left*. There were so many returning servicemen that the dinner also took place in the Town Hall, 19 July 1919.

134 *Below*. Dedication of the War Memorial, High Street. The memorial was unveiled on 7 May 1921 by General Lord Home. *See also* illustration 20.

135 *Right*. Remembrance Day, 11 November 1927.

136 The town band and members of the Territorials parading in Church Street on Remembrance Sunday. Note the cottages where Barnards Court now stands. The house on the left was for many years the home of the popular but eccentric local actress Mary Steiner. Cambridge House, currently used as the Magistrates' Court, was for many years Miss Gowlett's school, but during the 1950s and 1960s the County Library had its home there.

137 VE Day parade, High Street, 1945. Note the tape on the windows to prevent glass shattering during bombing.

People and Events

138 George Stacey Gibson and his family shaped Saffron Walden in the 19th century. They owned many of the pubs and most of the maltings. Gibson was a wealthy landowner, with strong banking and brewing interests. A local Quaker and benefactor of the town, he was also a keen photographer, and an amateur botanist of some note, who wrote the first *Flora of Essex* (1862). He was also instrumental in bringing the railway into Saffron Walden, building the Boys' British School and providing land for both the Friends' School and the Teacher Training College.

139 *Left.* Moat Farm, Clavering, where Camille Holland was brutally murdered by Samuel Dougal in 1899. The small white cross in the foreground indicates where police found her body in 1903, her grave is in the Radwinter Road cemetery. This sensational murder was the subject of a book by F. Tennyson Jesse.

140 *Below left.* Dougal in police custody, being transferred between trains at Audley End station after his arrest. He was remanded at the local Petty Sessions in the Town Hall, but was tried in Chelmsford, where he was executed in July 1903.

141 *Below.* Declaration of Poll, Parliamentary Elections, 20 December 1910. Cecil Beck, the Liberal candidate, (on the left), won by a mere 40 votes more than Col. D.J. Proby, the Conservative candidate (on the right of the platform).

142 R.A. 'Rab' Butler, M.P. for the Saffron Walden constituency, speaking to supporters from the window of the Museum Street Conservative Club, 1935. He was elected with 19,669 votes compared to 9,663 votes gained by Mrs. Rackham, the Labour candidate. Butler pioneered the 1944 Education Act and was Home Secretary in Macmillan's cabinet. He was Member of Parliament for the Saffron Walden constituency for 36 years, and Master of Trinity College, Cambridge for 13 years.

143 Heckling 'Rab' Butler outside the Corn Exchange during the General Election of 1951.

144 Floral arch erected in London Road to mark Queen Victoria's Silver Jubilee, in 1862. The arch was situated near the junction with Borough Lane and Audley End Road. The photograph looks towards the fields that became part of the County High School playing fields.

145 Hill House, High Street, decorated for the Coronation of Edward VII. The trees in High Street had just been planted.

146 Memorial parade for King Edward VII, Market Hill, 1910. Postmen, firemen and town councillors processing up Market Hill to the church.

147 Proclamation of the accession of King George V to the throne, 10 May 1910. Parading past the local councillors on the platform are firemen and postmen, with members of the Territorials at the front.

148 *Above*. King Street decorated for the Coronation of King George V, 1911, with the *Hoops* public house on the right. A newspaper report of 1775 tells the story of 11 fen workmen who offered a barmaid at the *Hoops* sixpence each to fetch all the beer they could drink. If they tired her out she would have to pay for their drink, but if she tired them, they would pay her. She accepted the bet and drew 517 single pints, and walked 12 miles from their room to the tap, but won the bet.

149 *Right*. Celebrations for the Coronation of King George V in the Market Place, 1911.

150 *Above right*. A children's tea-party in St Mary's School playground to celebrate the coronation, 1953. Similar parties were held all over the town.

151 *Above*. Empire Day, May 1913. Empire Day originally marked Queen Victoria's birthday when every child in the Market Place received an orange and a bun.

152 *Above right*. Empire Day, *c*.1913. The photograph was taken from the Corn Exchange roof which gives it an unusual perspective across the front of Stebbing Leverett's outfitters, and Emson Tanner's, now Eaden Lilleys.

153 *Right*. Shoppers in the Market Place observed two minutes' silence when the death of King George VI was announced in 1952.

154 *Above*. The Board of Guardians of the Union Workhouse (later St. James' Hospital, Radwinter Road), taken before 1930. The guardians were responsible for the administration of the workhouse. *Left to right, back row*: F.M. Furze; David Miller; ?; ?; D. Welch; ?; ? W. Thomason; H.C. Stallard; J.E. Tetlow; Tom Avery; *middle*: ?, James Clark; ?; ?; Alfred Pitstow; Ernest Hart; Rev. T.P. Conyers-Barker; J.A. Raven; Rev. G.E.A. Whitworth; Rev. M.R. Swabey; Frank Foster; H. Wiseman; J. Spencer-Smith; Stanley Reed; Dr. S.R. Richardson; Percy Wright (Clerk); *front row*: H.C. Merton; ?; A.S. Bathropp; H.J. Drage; ?; Mrs. Warren; Mrs. Salter; F.S.H. Judd; Rev. H.G. Brabant Smith; B.C. Custerson; Mrs. M.D. Midgley; Mrs. C. Custerson; Mrs. Luddington; Miss Ruse (clerk's assistant); Mrs. Lang (Matron).

155 *Right*. Churching the Mayor, Market Place, 1926. J.W. Pateman was the mayor, with the mayoral chain round his neck; the town clerk, wearing the short wig was W.M. Adams. A.N. Dunscombe, the Borough Accountant, is on the right. The ceremony recalls the annual election of the mayor by the local guild, which met in the muniment room over the south porch of the church.

156 Saffron Walden Corporation, 1937. *Left to right, back row*: A.M. Dunsombe (Borough Accountant); P.L. Allen (Representing Borough Treasurer); Coun. C.E. Day; Coun. H. Collar; Coun. H. Tanner; H.A. Cook (Borough Surveyor); Dr. S.R. Richardson (Medical Officer); *middle row*: A.C. Marsh (Sgt.-at-Mace); Coun. G.O. Bradley; Coun. S.S. Wilson; Coun. A.R. Ray; Coun. C.G. Engelman, Coun. G.C. Maberly; Coun. Miss M.E. Midgley; Coun. C.B. Rowntree; Coun. A.J. Dix; Coun. H.P. Lawrence; F. Sewell (Mace-Bearer); *front row*: Alderman P.G. Cowell; C.S.D. Wade; Linton T. Thorp, K.C.; The Mayor, Alderman E. Rooke; The Deputy Mayor, Alderman J. Custerson; G.A.E. Ruck (Town Clerk); Alderman A. Titchmarsh.

157 The district meeting of the Independent Order of Rechabites, Saffron Walden Tent 3741, Essex District, no. 50. The picture was posed in the burial ground at the rear of the Friends' Meeting House, in the High Street. Some of the gravestones are clearly visible in the foreground.

158 *Above*. Mayor Ellis Rooke with Field-Marshal Montgomery in Castle Street on their way to the official opening of the Anglo-American Playing Fields, 1955.

159 *Above right*. When the Madgate Slade flooded in September 1968, Bridge End Gardens were submerged in water.

160 *Right*. Bridge End flooded in 1968. Miss Gatesman wading to her house. Note the ladder at Ernie Westwood's. Although the Madgate Slade is often little more than a trickle, Sir Edward de Bohun was drowned there in 1333. It also flooded severely in 1903 when people had to be rescued from the upstairs windows.

161 *Above left*. The aftermath of the fire at the *Rose and Crown*, Boxing Day, 1969. Eleven people died in the fire.

162 *Above right*. Fire at Rumsey's furniture shop at the junction of High Street and King Street.

163 *Below*. Rally for peace in Northern Ireland, November 1976. Carrying the banner at the head of the rally are local Quaker, farmer and natural history writer, Robert Mays, and Ernest Effer, a tireless campaigner on civil liberties and environmental issues.

Leisure and Sport

Edwin Drew's Pageant Poems.

Author of the Commemoration Poems of
Winchester, Colchester, Bath and Cardiff Pageants.

Saffron Walden Pageant.

MAY, 1910.

DEDICATED TO' THE ANCIENT TOWN OF
SAFFRON WALDEN.

The Author has had the Patronage of Their Most Gracious
Majesties our King and Queen and many other Royalties.

'TIS well, with all its wealth of old renown,
  That SAFFRON WALDEN, famed historic town
Should rise in all the dignity of age,
In Pageantry, so beauteous to engage.

In early centuries she held her own,
In Peace and War, well was her spirit shewn
And on the story of our island told,
In tender moment or in passage bold.

Amid fair scenes of calm and quietude,
Old Saffron Walden, with her power renewed,
In conscious strength her ancient lore displays
Depicting doings of departed days.

The warrior grandly aids the glowing feast,
Sweet lady, gallant knight, and pious priest
With peasantry, with picture, word and song.
Before delighted vision pass along.

Thus Past and Present splendidly unite,
The far off times are here before our sight,
And Saffron Walden shews artistic taste
To crown the fame by which her brow is
                                    graced.

————————

PRICE ONE PENNY.

Of the Author, EDWIN DREW, ir Saffron Walden, or at
162 Kentish Town Road, London.

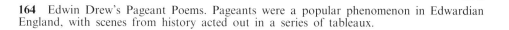

164 Edwin Drew's Pageant Poems. Pageants were a popular phenomenon in Edwardian
England, with scenes from history acted out in a series of tableaux.

165 The Saffron Walden Pageant, 1910. Tableaux depicting the funeral of Geoffrey de Mandeville.

166 Fair on the Common, *c*.1910. Fairs have contributed to the economic life of the town since at least 1248, providing opportunities to buy and sell. In 1514 a charter included a licence to 'have and hold for evermore one Fayr at owre Towne aforeseyd every yer duryng iiij dayes in the fest of the xj^m virg^s'. The Feast of the 11,000 Virgins, or St Ursula, was celebrated in October, but the Walden Fair seems to have been held in early November.

167 Floral Fête, 1907. One of the themes of the fête that year was the depiction of gypsies.

168 May Day 'Nut scramble' outside Owen Baker's grocer's shop in Debden Road, 1911. Groups of small girls carrying garlands would go from house to house singing a May Day carol: the first verse went:

'I, I have been a-rambling all this night
And some part of this day
and now, returning back again,
I have brought you a garland gay.'

169 *Above*. Saffron Walden Football Club, winners of the Essex Junior Cup, 1907. *Left to right, back row*: ?; Frank Housden; Stephen Reed; Charles Green; Bill Cornell; Oscar Whitehead; Walter Parish, referee (from Colchester); Fred Green. *Centre*: H. Dennis; Henry Housden; J.P. Whitlow. *Front row*: Sam Legerton; P.L. Allen; Jim Whitehead; H Whitehead; R.A Strong.

170 *Above right*. Would-be swimmers from the Boys British School in the public swimming baths, 1911. Built on a site previously occupied by Nunn's ironmongers and given by Miss Mary Gibson, the baths opened in 1910. The pool was supplied with water from a deep bore well sunk by Jabez Gibson in 1836. The boys are shown at the 'deep end' (6 feet 3 inches deep). After the baths were demolished, Market Walk was built in its place.

171 *Right*. The Liberal Tennis Club at the corner of Station Street and Station Road. Custersons then Ridgeons had their depot there for many years, and flats have recently been built on the site. The old engine sheds can be seen in the background. *Left to right, back row*: The Methodist Minister, Jealous; Bosomworth; Watts; Mrs. Hart; Bert Start; Charles Spurge; Barbara Smith; Frank Furlong; Mrs. Start. *middle row*: ?; Miss Furlong; M.E. Hart; Jacques; Ethel Ramsey; Ruby Palmer; Horsepool; Iris Miller; Gilbert Foan; F. Bacon; *front row*: ?; Percy Wright; Mrs. Julius Green; Bernard Choppen; ?; Frank Wilkerson; 1912.

172 Saffron Walden's cricket team, photographed after the successful year in 1921 in which they won 17 matches, drew 3 and lost none. *Left to right, back row*: S. Day; H.R. Downham; C. Reed; *third row*: H.G. Eggett (umpire); P. Whitehead; B.A. Myhill; J.P. Whitlow; E.C.F. Land; E. Hurry; R.A. Strong; T. Marshall (scorer); *second row*: C.R. Downham (Capt.), H.J. Cheffins (President); E.H. Cro (vice-capt.); *front row*: J. Ketteridge; A. Kitteridge; Cowell.

173 The Common, *c.*1920. The cricket pavilion on the left was removed to the Anglo-American playing fields in the 1950s. The temporary hedging in the middle of the common was erected to protect the cricket pitches during the winter months.

174 Soldiers of the North or South Staffordshires with the Pitstow family of bell-ringers, 1915. Leonard Pitstow, Harold Pitstow, Mrs. Pitstow, Ernest Pitstow and, on the extreme right, Hilda Pitstow. The Pitstow family has a long tradition of church bell ringing. In 1893 four members of the family were among a team which rang 5,024 changes in 3 hours 14 minutes.

175 Saffron Walden Town Band, 1912. *Left to right* (*back row*): Frank King, Fred Pursey, Charles Wren, Frank Braybrooke. (*third row*): Sid Wyatt, Arthur Badman, Albert Housden, Arthur Martin, Doug King, Sid Bowtell, Tom Lacey. (*second row*): Tom Marshall, Fred J. Pitstow, Fred Housden, Alfred E. Pitstow, Harry Pursey, Herbert Ryan, George Braybrooke. (*front row*): Alf Walls, Arthur Simpson, Bill Stubbings, Harold White, Jack Day, Bill Bradman.

176 Saffron Walden Cinema, High Street, 1912. The ceremony to mark the completion of the building by Rooke and Sons of Cambridge. It was the town's first purpose built cinema, although Andrew Dix presented films in the Central Hall. Originally owned by Ernest Smith and then by Tozer and Lindsell, it could seat 420 people. In August 1950 the building burnt down and a new cinema was built.

177 Saffron Walden Motor Cycle Club in the late 1920s early 1930s. *Left to right*: Arthur Downham; Ted Peasgood; Webb; Goss; ?; Wilfred Choppen; Reg Long; Peplow; Ken Archer. *Left to right*: Bikes 4 and 5 were water-cooled Scott's, bikes 7 and 9 were BSAs.

178 Roller skating in fancy dress inside the old Corn Exchange, before 1914.

179 Carnival float on the theme of the Mazer bowl, *c.*1925. Made in about 1507 and given by Margaret Breychman, the bowl was shown to Samuel Pepys, who wrote: 'They brought me a drink in a brown bowl, tipt with silver, which I drank off, and at the bottom was a picture of the Virgin and the Child in her arms, done in silver'. The bowl was sold in 1929 to pay for repairs to the almshouses, and is currently on display at the British Museum.

Bibliography

Bassett, S. R., *Saffron Walden; excavations and research 1972-80* (1982)

The Book of the Foundation of Walden Abbey. Transcribed and translated by C.H. Emson, in *Essex Review*, 45, 46, 47 (1936-38)

Braybrooke, Richard, Lord, *The History of Audley End and Saffron Walden* (1836)

Fox, C., *The Archaeology of the Cambridge Region* (1923)

Gesta Stephani, edited and translated by K.R. Potter, with new introduction and notes by R.H.C. Davis (1976)

Harrison, W., *The Description of England* (1577)

Monteith, D., *Saffron Walden and Its Environs: a study in the development of a landscape*. MA thesis, University of Leicester (1958)

Morant, P., *The History and Antiquities of the County of Essex* (1768)

Rowntree, C.B., *Saffron Walden Then and Now* (1951)

White, M., *Saffron Walden's History: a Chronological Compilation* (1991)

Index

Roman numerals refer to pages in the Introduction, and arabic numerals to individual illustrations.